INTO Wild Florida

BLACKBIRCH®
PRESS

THOMSON
GALE

San Diego • Detroit • New York • San Francisco • Cleveland • New Haven, Conn. • Waterville, Maine • London • Munich

THOMSON
GALE

For more information, contact
The Gale Group, Inc.
27500 Drake Rd.
Farmington Hills, MI 48331-3535
Or you can visit our Internet site at http://www.gale.com

LIBRARY OF CONGRESS CATALOGING-IN-PUBLICATION DATA

Pascoe, Elaine,
Into wild Florida / Elaine Pascoe, book editor.
    p. cm. — (The Jeff Corwin Experience)
: Jeff Corwin takes you along on his travels through Wild Florida
Includes bibliographical references and index.
  ISBN: 1567119506 (lib.: alk. paper)
      141030177X (pbk.: alk. paper)
  1. Let's explore Florida —Florida—wildlife—Juvenile literature. [1. Seminoles,snakes, swamps —Florida—.] I. Pascoe, Elaine. II. Series.

  F311.3 .P67 2004
  975.9 —dc21

Printed in China
10 9 8 7 6 5 4 3 2 1

E ver since I was a kid, I dreamed about traveling around the world, visiting exotic places, and seeing all kinds of incredible animals. And now, guess what? That's exactly what I get to do!

Yes, I am incredibly lucky. But, you don't have to have your own television show on Animal Planet to go off and explore the natural world around you. I mean, I travel to Madagascar and the Amazon and all kinds of really cool places—but I don't need to go that far to see amazing wildlife up close. In fact, I can find thousands of incredible critters right here, in my own backyard—or in my neighbor's yard (he does get kind of upset when he finds me crawling around in the bushes, though). The point is, no matter where you are, there's fantastic stuff to see in nature. All you have to do is look.

I love snakes, for example. Now, I've come face to face with the world's most venomous vipers—some of the biggest, some of the strongest, and some of the rarest. But I've also found an amazing variety of snakes just traveling around my home state of Massachussetts. And I've taken trips to preserves, and state parks, and national parks —and in each place I've enjoyed unique and exciting plants and animals. So, if I can do it, you can do it, too (except for the hunting venomous snakes part!). So, plan a nature hike with some friends. Organize some projects with your science teacher at school. Ask mom and dad to put a state or a national park on the list of things to do on your next family vacation. Build a bird house. Whatever. But get out there.

As you read through these pages and look at the photos, you'll probably see how jazzed I get when I come face to face with beautiful animals. That's good. I want you to feel that excitement. And I want you to remember that—even if you don't have your own TV show—you can still experience the awesome beauty of nature almost anywhere you go—any day of the week. I only hope that I can help bring that awesome power and beauty a little closer to you. Enjoy!

Jeff Corwin

INTO
Wild Florida

It's a place just filled with surprising creatures. Serpents of all kinds. Water moccasins. Legendary sea creatures. Crocodilians of all sizes. A natural world more exciting than any amusement park.

I'm Jeff Corwin.
Welcome to Florida.

Starting in North Florida, take a little trip with me as we move south, towards the Everglades, where I hope to meet a real swamp thing.

Homosassa Springs

Here's where we're going first.

The Florida we've come to find is not that state famous for its highway system or its amusement parks or tourist attractions. We've come to find the Florida of the past, that Florida first experienced by those explorers who came here hundreds of years ago. Spanish explorers like Ponce de Leon. He came all the way over from Spain to find the Fountain of Youth. Did he find it? No, because he's dead. Other explorers came here as well. They came here for the natural wealth of Florida, in search of gold. And did they find gold? I don't know. But I do know they encountered *natural* gold, locked up in the wildlife of this place. And that's why we're here in Florida, to experience its wildlife.

This is one of the critters we're going to meet...

That's a Seminole chickee behind me.

We'll start our journey in north Florida, near Homosassa Springs. Before the Spanish claimed Florida, this land was home to a variety of native tribes. Almost all of them disappeared, wiped out by the Europeans. Today, the most dominant Florida tribe is the Seminole Indian Nation, which once claimed a large part of Florida as their home.

The traditional Seminole home is called a *chickee*. In the Seminole language, chickee means "my home," and this is where they lived. Chickees are made from thatch that is intricately woven together.

Aren't these eastern indigos gorgeous?

Here is the first creature I found. Look at this. How is that for a gorgeous snake? This guy is the eastern indigo snake, getting the name indigo

LOOK AT THIS!

A group of Florida Seminole pose in front of their village in 1910.

The Florida Seminole were left alone for nearly seventy-five years after the Seminole Wars ended. The government tried to bribe them to move west, but the offers were ignored. Finally, in 1932, the Seminole agreed to move to land in central and southern Florida. Some became cattle herders. Others worked for wages. Today, the Seminole live on six reservations in Florida.

This snake has an incredible purple glow.

A long body and a narrow head mean you're looking at a Colubrid.

snake from that beautiful sheen, that sort of purpley glow and that iridescent shine you see across its scales.

Now, if you want to identify the family of this creature, the family of snakes it belongs to, just look at its shape. It has a long body, a narrow head, and usually what that means is the snake you're studying, at least in North America, is a Colubrid, one of the largest family of snakes. Thousands of representative snakes belong to the Colubridae family. And this snake, the indigo, is the longest Colubrid you'll find in North America.

In fact, it's the longest snake living in North America. They can push 8, sometimes even 9 feet in length. Now, indigos are voracious predators. All sorts of creatures make up the diet of this animal, from lizards and amphibians, like frogs, to other snakes and rodents.

The indigo is the longest snake in North America.

What's interesting about these indigo snakes is that they're winter breeders. They begin breeding in November. So while other snakes are hibernating, these guys are mating. And you can see why the indigo snake is potentially a very popular animal for those who collect snakes. But again, it's important to remember that this creature is protected as a species. It is protected by the Homosassa Springs Wildlife State Park.

Homosassa Springs is a state conservation area, and is also home to one of Florida's most famous creatures. When Christopher Columbus sailed to the New World, his ship's log recorded that the crew sighted mermaids, but that they weren't quite as handsome as in the paintings.

These creatures are clearly not elephants, but they do share a distant ancestry with African and Asian elephants. These are manatees. If you look at how they feed, you can see a similarity to elephants. Because their lips are actually prehensiled, they function like a digit and what they're reminding me of is an elephant. If you ever looked at the tip of an elephant's trunk,

Look at this guy's lips—they're a lot like an elephant's trunk.

you'll see that it is very digit like when it reaches up and pulls on vegetation. These animals are doing something very similar. They're able to pull their lips together to pull food inside.

I wish you could feel the flesh of this animal. It's smooth, but it has little burrs, and it's covered with hair, lots of hair. If you look at its muzzle, you can see that it is covered by thousands and

The flesh of this animal is incredible. It's smooth, but has little burrs.

thousands of whiskers, and those whiskers are used to feel. But what's amazing is that sailors hundreds of years ago, when they saw these animals, thought that these marine mammals were half-fish, half-female. That's

Can you believe sailors thought this face was actually a beautiful mermaid?

why they called them mermaids. And well, of course it's just a legend. Mermaids don't really exist, but legends are pretty cool.

Now, let's move towards south Florida.

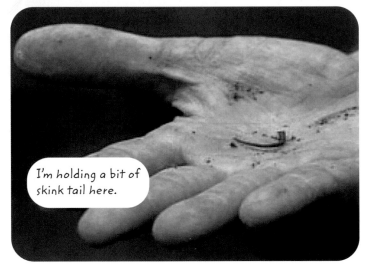

I'm holding a bit of skink tail here.

I'm here, just outside of Jacksonville, with my friend J.J., in this nice tract of old forest. It's a good place for critters, I hear. There are a lot of small lizards, and they are being eaten by larger stuff.

I saw something move over there. Oh, a skink. A skink saw me coming and he went in defense mode. He dropped his tail. It's a great defense; you lose your tail and then you run off and you regenerate a new one.

Aren't skinks cool?

In a couple of weeks, you'll start seeing a little stub there coming back. But it's a great defense, because other animals focus by this bright, twitching tail.

Tons of skinks here in Florida.

Florida water moccasins are beautiful animals, but they are dangerous.

And, over here, a water moccasin. That's a beautiful, beautiful Florida water moccasin. We need to be careful, because this is a venomous animal. Isn't it great though? You can see the way he just blends in. Spectacular camouflage. He's not even crawling away because he's hoping that I'm just going to walk right over him. The thing is I have to move slowly, because he's looking for rapid movement.

When you hold this snake, you can feel that sort of leathery texture. That color, it almost looks like tanned leather. Hence the word "moccasin," like the shoe that a Native American might have worn years and years ago. And of course, you know the other name for these guys? Cottonmouth.

If you notice the coloration here, what's really special about this species, the Florida water moccasin, is that you can actually see the bands more. See that? They're much more vivid. Especially if you look at the belly. You can really see where those bands go from the dorsal scales to the ventral scales, right?

This snake feels like tanned leather when you hold it.

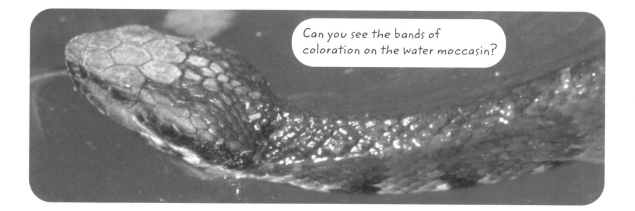

Can you see the bands of coloration on the water moccasin?

And, it gets the name "cottonmouth" by this. See how white that mouth is? That white flesh?

When he's frightened, he sort of coils up, pulls his head in, knocks his mouth back, and anything that's going to come trampling him says, "Whoa, I have to stop." Because his first line of defense is actually camouflage. He's master at blending in.

This snake is probably up here on land because even though it's not bordering a body of water, it is a pretty damp place. But probably the best reason why he's here is because of prey. This creature has everything from mice lizards and frogs to eat in this area.

I'll let him go now, so we can move on.

See how white that mouth is? That's why they call them cottonmouths.

About 120 miles to the south of the Jacksonville forest is a slice of pristine Florida habitat, and it's only minutes from Orlando. It's Lake Tohopekaliga.

Every time I walk here, an intense organic odor comes from somewhere in this area. No, it's not what you think.

This lake is very cool, but it's got a funky smell!

It's coming from this lake—extremely organic, lots of natural gases—not from me, but from the lake. As I walk, the bubbles come up, methane and stuff like that. Now, there's a very interesting study being conducted here. It's a cooperative study. We have researchers from the University of Florida working here, looking at all sorts of stuff. And one of the things they're looking at is a very interesting creature.

What is probably coming to your mind is an eel. You're thinking eels, right? Wrong. Although they are aquatic, they are not eels; they're not fish. These are amphibians. In fact, they're the largest salamander-like animals you will ever see in this part of the world. These are sirens, an extraordinary salamander. Really, really neat creature. They love to eat crayfish. And I'm going to release them as well. Very fish-like, but again, looks can be deceiving. Look at these amphibians. Look at the size of that guy.

No, it's not an eel! It's an amphibian. A salamander, actually.

This is just going to blow you away. Get ready for a natural zenith. We've come all the way for this. A snail. Hey! Hey, don't put this book down. There's a reason why we've come to see the snail. Because this is a snail that's unique to this region. It's called the apple snail. And although it's just a gastropod, just a mollusk, there are some amazing things about this snail which I'm going to show you.

First of all, there's a very unique feature to this apple snail. See that? It comes with its own antenna. It has this antenna because it's a part of a very important scientific study.

Is this the most amazing apple snail you've ever seen?

Now you're wondering, who would fund a study like this? Don't they have more to do than study apple snails? Well, there's a lot to learn from an apple snail. These creatures play a very important role in this complex ecosystem, and perhaps the greatest role they play is as a source of prey to one very important bird of prey, the snail kite. Snail kites feed almost exclusively on these creatures. So by better understanding the population of this animal, you can understand the population of those creatures that depend on this animal as a resource. All creatures, whether big or small, have a place in the ecosystems that they live in.

This guy is a snail kite. He likes eating apple snails.

How do you stop this thing?

We're still headed south. Ahead of us lie the legendary Everglades. Hard to believe that here in the Big Cypress Swamp, we're only an hour from Miami. But the Everglades cover a huge area, nearly 4,000 square miles, half as big as my home state of Massachusetts. It can be an intimidating place. Even the famous American naturalist John Muir felt a little uneasy about exploring here. What was he afraid of? Just one creature, the alligator.

In the Big Cypress Seminole Indian Reservation, I'm hoping for a friendly gator encounter. I hope the gator has the same idea.

And here's the nest. Look at this right here. The reason why the female has left it probably has to do with the extreme floods we've had in this region. Now, this is a wetland. It's used to having a lot of water. But there's been a lot of water lately and the water has lifted up a couple of feet. And when these nests are covered for more than twelve hours under water, they're dead. So let's see if we can find, let's see....Oh, look at this. Look at this. A beautiful, beautiful, alligator egg. Beautiful alligator egg. Let me look at it up to the light.

I can actually see the embryo curled up in there. Now, I want to mark it because I need to know what side is the top. So when I place it in the container, if I place it upside down, it can shift things around, mess up the little bubble of air in there, and potentially kill the embryo. So I have to be very careful as I transplant these eggs from the nest to this container. It's lined with very, very soft peat moss. All right, egg number one. I put them in here like this. A lot of eggs in here, a lot of eggs.

There's a gator nest here somewhere...

I can actually see the embryo curled up inside.

I need to know which side is the top.

So why are we doing this? Why are we excavating this nest? Because, we have to remember, where were alligators twenty or thirty years ago? They were this close to extinction. We have to do everything we can to conserve this species. A nest is in jeopardy, and we're salvaging the eggs. Let's go.

I'll drop these eggs off at an incubation facility that's run by the Seminoles. Then we'll see if we can find another gator nest, maybe one that's already hatched out.

Right there is an active alligator nest. It's covered by all these little hatchlings, probably no more than a few days old. Off in the distance is the mother. The babies are sitting on the mother's muzzle. If you want an example of how good gator mothers are when it comes to rearing their offspring and protecting their babies from predators, just check out the head of that animal. She has a crown constructed, not of jewels or metal, but of baby gators hanging out there.

Can you see the baby gators in there?

She's looking right at me. She's not taking her eyes off of me. What I want to do is sort of check out this nest. I just want to see if there's anything in there. Maybe there are some eggs that haven't hatched. Look at that; it's like a compost heap. Ooh, look at that. There's an egg right there. See that? That's an egg.

Mama's looking right at me with a baby on her head!

Gator eggs are really leathery.

Yikes!

Here's an actual gator egg that's hatched. And that little baby ripped through that egg shell with a caruncle. A caruncle is an egg tooth. You don't get one, but baby gators do. That way, the caruncle can actually rip through that leathery layer of the shell.

Somewhere in this swamp, there's a seventy-year-old gator that's enormous. So that's where we're headed.

LOOK AT THIS!

Did you know that the sex of an alligator is determined by the temperature at which the egg is incubated? It's true. Eggs incubated at about 85 degrees Fahrenheit (29.4 degrees Celsius) produce females. Eggs incubated in the low 90s (around 33 degrees Celsius) produce males.

Scientists and researchers have spent a lot of time learning about alligator reproduction. That's because thirty years ago alligators were endangered. Many people believed this unique reptile would never recover. Luckily, a combined effort by the U.S. Fish and Wildlife Service and state wildlife agencies in the South saved these unique animals. The Endangered Species Act prohibited alligator hunting, allowing the species to rebound in numbers in many areas where it had been depleted. As the alligator began to make a comeback, states established alligator population monitoring programs and used this information to make sure alligator numbers continued to increase. In 1987, the Fish and Wildlife Service pronounced the American alligator fully recovered and consequently moved the animal off the list of endangered species.

Here is a great animal. She is sleeping and purring like a baby. But she's a great actress. And the Academy Award goes to Felis concolor, or the American mountain lion.

Aren't mountain lions gorgeous?

One of the first explorers to spot this animal was the Spaniard Álvar Nuñez Cabeza de Vaca, who thought he had sighted an actual African lion. Of course, he'd never seen a lion before, but he'd heard a description of that big cat, so he figured this must be it. Now clearly, this animal isn't a wild one. It's used in educational programs here at Billy's Swamp Safari. But I still have to respect it, because if it has a bad day, even though it likes people, I'm in trouble.

If this cat seems a little comatose, it's because it's by nature nocturnal. And this one insists on getting its beauty sleep. So perhaps you're wondering why are we looking at a mountain lion here in Florida? Because there is a race of mountain lions, called the Florida panther, which you can only find living in this part of the world. They're very rare. There are only about sixty of them living in the wild, and if we want to get a good feeling of what makes the Florida panther so special, we have to explore its cousin, which lives up in the north.

Florida panthers are a rare sight.

These guys like staying low in the cover of tall grass.

Now, why are the differences between the northern race and the southern race unique to Florida? Possibly it has something to do with the vegetation. It's very dense habitat you've got to deal with, slicing through razor sharp palms and grasses. You don't have a lot of tall forest, especially in southern Florida. So a big-bodied animal would encounter more of an obstacle when moving through habitat. But today, the physical differences between the panther and the mountain lion are harder to point out. That's because the true Florida panther was hunted to near extinction.

Look at those incredible panther eyes.

And when the more common mountain lion was brought in to increase the population, a true Florida panther became even harder to find. Today, almost all of the big cats in Florida are not pure panther, but they do share many of the same traits.

Look at the size of these paws. Very little sound is generated from this creature as it moves, and that's very important when it comes to leaping or pouncing.

These huge paws make the panther's movements very quiet.

Want a ride in my swamp buggy?

If you have a swamp buggy like this one, you can drive for miles and never leave the boundaries of the Big Cypress Swamp. Everything's all flooded, so if we want to find some more snakes, we have to go to some drier habitat. We're actually moving off of Seminole land and into an area called the Bush Wildlife Sanctuary.

Okay, look. Tucked underneath this layer of pinecones is a beautiful, beautiful serpent. That beautiful face is sticking right out, its tongue tickling the air. That triangular shape and those divots are a clue to us that we are dealing with a viper. Just look at the tail. A rattle. So we have an eastern diamondback rattlesnake. First, I'm just going to secure the back end of her tail so I can work her safely. I've got her out of strike range so she can't strike me. And now I can hold her up like this so you can have a look at this gorgeous snake.

See the triangular head shape? That means viper!

Look at the size of it. Look how stocky this creature is. She's got two very large fangs to the front, large venom glands, Duvernoy's glands, and can deliver a copious amount of venom. Now what's neat about the venom of this animal is that it is not only designed to be lethal, it's also designed to liquefy, to dissolve the flesh, to promote the digestive process of the prey that this creature is eating, such as a rodent. So let's place this creature back into this little area, where we discovered it, and see what else we can find here in the Bush Wildlife Sanctuary.

Look what I found!

Here is a beautiful, beautiful serpent. Look at this. A serpent famous for its beauty, and famous for its toxicity, its venom. A snake you have to be very careful with. It's a coral snake. Very venomous.

Look at the colors of this beautiful (and very venomous) serpent.

I'm going to tell you a very happy story. It's about a ballerina wannabe. In my left hand, I've got the coral snake. It is the most venomous snake in the New World. And coral snakes practice aposematic coloration, bright warning colors that send a message, "Stay away, because I don't want to bite but if I do, you're up the creek without a paddle, buddy."

With the snake in my right hand, I'm being a lot more cavalier, because this is the scarlet king snake. And it practices aposematic coloration as well, but it's mimicry. It is hoping to confuse would-be predators by looking like the

highly dangerous coral snake. So how do you know the difference? It's all in the pattern. If you look at this coral snake, you'll see the red is touching the yellow. If you look at this scarlet king snake, the red is touching the black. And as we say: "Red touches black, friend to Jack. Red touches yellow, kill a fellow."

One thing about Florida, it's very wet. Tons of water. It's one of the wettest states in North America. You have a lot of natural limestone springs like this one, which snake their way through this habitat. Something interesting about all this water is that for hundreds of years, it's been a part of the folklore of this land. It's been a part of Native American folklore and even the ancient European folklore. For example, when Ponce de Leon came to Florida, he was in search of magical water, water containing properties that could reduce one's age. You know what I'm talking about: the Fountain of Youth.

It's croc against gator!

Here, I have both an alligator and a crocodile in my hands. A lot of people don't know the differences between alligators and crocodiles, so I thought I'd show you.

Both the alligator and the crocodile belong to the same group, called crocodilians, but there are many differences between the two. Alligators prefer more of a freshwater habitat. That's not to say that they won't venture into some brackish water, but they like slow moving streams. They like ponds just like this. The crocodile is much more adapted to survive in a marine environment. You find them living more to the coast. You find them living in estuarine type habitats. Now that's not to say these guys can't venture out of their usual habitats; there are places in Florida where you can find both alligators and crocodiles living together. But for the most part, alligators prefer the freshwater habitat, while crocs are more designed for a marine environment.

So, speaking of marine environment, look at the tails. What you'll notice is that on the crocodile, the scale-like plates, the scutes are much higher. The scutes are raised up on the tail and the surface between those scutes is much flatter, all right? While the alligator, you'll see the scutes are more pronounced, while the scutes along the side aren't raised, aren't fin-like as you see with the crocodile.

Now, here's the biggest differences between alligators and crocodiles. It is in the head region and what you'll notice is that the alligator has a very broad snout. Very broad. While the crocodile has a longer and more narrow snout.

See how much broader the snout on the right is?

It's only in this pristine habitat of Florida that you can see both alligators and crocodiles living together. Amazing stuff.

This is a very large alligator. His name is Superman, and of course, you can't come to Florida without seeing a gator. And you're looking at one of the largest ones living in the state of Florida. This guy is pushing near to 14 feet in length, he's a huge animal. Now, out in the wild, a gator this size is a rare sight indeed. You're looking at an animal that's probably somewhere between fifty and sixty years in age. And this guy's probably weighing somewhere between 800 to 1,000 pounds. It is a perfectly designed animal. Essentially, you're looking at one great, scaly eating machine. And in a mid-aged gator, it probably has somewhere around eighty teeth in its mouth. But this animal will grow teeth throughout its lifetime. And it will produce upwards of three thousand teeth.

Say hello to Superman!

Now I'm going to move in, but I want to move in very cautiously, very slowly. When this guy is in a bad mood, you might lose a leg, so you've got to be careful.

He's hissing.

That's the sign of agitation. That's the sound of a gator who says, "You're getting a little too close." What you're probably thinking is the number one defense for this creature is its teeth, which is true, this creature can bite. But coming in pretty close to its teeth is this animal's tail. It has a huge, muscular tail, and when this

This tail is a major weapon.

animal feels threatened, it will curl the tail back and whack forward. And a tail like this is strong enough to break your legs if it were to whack you. And just look at the girth of this tail. You see that's a very thick tail. A lot of energy is stored in this creature. Now in addition to being protected by that arsenal of teeth in its mouth and a macelike tail, which could snap the legs of any would-be predator, it's also protected by

Don't try this at home!

this skin, this dermis. It has a very thick hide, and inside each of these little divisions, are scale-like plates, the scutes. Bony-like structures.

Well, I hope you enjoyed our journey through Florida, and all the wonderful creatures from the manatees to the alligators to the snakes and the crocodiles. It's a great place, a very important part of North America's natural history. I look forward to seeing you again on our next great adventure!

Glossary

amphibian an animal that lives in water as a baby and on land as an adult

compost a mixture made up of decayed organic matter and used for fertilizing land

conservation preservation or protection

dermis skin

digits fingers and toes

dorsal located on the back of an animal

ecosystem a community of organisms and its environment that function as a unit

embryo an animal in the early stages of development

endangered threatened with extinction

estuarine related to an area where the ocean meets the lower end of a river

folklore traditional customs, tales, or sayings

habitat the place or environment in which a plant or animal usually grows

lethal deadly

muzzle the projecting jaws and nose of an animal

naturalist a field biologist

nocturnal active at night

predator an animal that lives by killing and eating other animals

prehensile adapted for grasping by wrapping around

prey an animal taken by a predator as food

pristine pure and unspoiled by civilization

regenerate re-grow a body part

reservation land set aside by the U.S. government for Native Americans

scute a large scale or plate on the body

species kind, type

venomous poisonous

ventral located on the belly or lower surface of an animal's body

zenith highest point

Index

Alligator, 26-31, 42-45
  caruncle, 30
  vs. crocodile, 42-43
  eggs, 27-29
  nest, 27-29
  "Superman," 44
Amphibians, 11, 23
Aposematic coloration, 38, 39

Big Cypress Swamp, 26, 36
Billy's Swamp Safari, 32
Bush Wildlife Sanctuary, 36, 38

Cabeza de Vaca, 32
Camouflage, 18
Columbus, Christopher, 13
Crocodile, 42-43
Crocodilians, 4, 42

Defense mode
  alligator, 45
  skink, 16
  water moccasin, 21
Digits, 13-14

Ecosystem, 25
Elephants, 13
Endangered Species Act, The, 31
Everglades, 6, 26
Extinction, 28, 34

Fountain of Youth, 7, 41
Frogs, 11, 20

Gastropod, 24

Habitats, 42

Homosassa Springs Wildlife State
  Park, 8, 11, 12-13

Incubation, 28, 31

Lake Tohopekaliga
  methane in, 23
  odor of, 22
Limestone springs, 41
Lizards
  as prey, 11, 20
  skink, 16-18

Manatee, 13-15
Mountain lion, American (Felis concolor), 32
Muir, John, 26
Muzzle
  alligator, 28
  manatee, 14-15

Panther, Florida, 33-35
Ponce de Leon, 7, 41
Predators
  diamondback rattlesnake, 38
  indigo snake, 11
  snail kite, 25
  water moccasin, 20
Prey
  frogs, 11, 20
  lizards, 11, 20
  rodents, 11, 38
  snail, apple, 24-25

Regeneration, 17

Salamander, 23

Seminole
  chickee, 8
  incubation facility, 28
  Indian Nation, 8
  Indian Reservation, Big Cypress,
    26, 36
  Wars, 9
Skink, 16
Snail, apple, 24-25
Snail kite, 25
Snakes
  Colubrid(ae), 10
  coral, 39-40
  cottonmouth, 18, 20-21
  indigo, eastern, 8, 10-11
  rattlesnake, eastern diamondback,
    37-38
  scarlet king, 40
  venom of, 18, 38
  viper, 37
  water moccasin, 5, 18-19
"Superman" (alligator), 44-45
Swamp buggy, 36

University of Florida, 23
U.S. Fish and Wildlife Service, 31

Viper. *See* snakes.